MW01101544

APPLESAUCE

by Gretchen Will Mayo

Reading consultant: Susan Nations, M.Ed., author/literacy coach/consultant

Please visit our web site at: **www.earlyliteracy.cc**
For a free color catalog describing Weekly Reader® Early Learning Library's
list of high-quality books, call 1-877-445-5824 (USA) or 1-800-387-3178 (Canada).
Weekly Reader® Early Learning Library's fax: (414) 336-0164.

Library of Congress Cataloging-in-Publication Data

Mayo, Gretchen.
    Applesauce / by Gretchen Will Mayo.
       p. cm. — (Where does our food come from?)
    Summary: Describes how apples are grown and made into the popular food, applesauce.
    Includes bibliographical references and index.
    ISBN 0-8368-4064-X (lib. bdg.)
    ISBN 0-8368-4071-2 (softcover)
    1. Cookery—Juvenile literature. 2. Applesauce—Juvenile literature. [1. Apples.
  2. Applesauce.] I. Title.
TX652.5.M3545   2004
641.6'411—dc22   2003061001

This edition first published in 2004 by
Weekly Reader® Early Learning Library
330 West Olive Street, Suite 100
Milwaukee, WI 53212 USA

Editor: JoAnn Early Macken
Art direction, cover and layout design: Tammy Gruenewald
Photo research: Diane Laska-Swanke

Photo credits: Cover (main), title, pp. 4, 5, 6, 7, 8, 9, 10, 11, 13, 14, 15, 16, 17, 18, 19, 20, 21 © Gregg Andersen;
cover (background) © Diane Laska-Swanke; p. 12 © Gibson Stock Photography

Printed in the United States of America

1 2 3 4 5 6 7 8 9 08 07 06 05 04

Table of Contents

Apples and applesauce are healthy treats.

Healthy and Sweet

Some people get to pick apples from their own trees. Crisp apples fresh from a tree taste sweet. Applesauce is also a great fruit treat. Many people make it at home.

What a yummy way to give your body vitamins! Apples have vitamins A and C. Apples have minerals, too. Minerals help your body build bones and muscles.

Applesauce makes a good snack after school.

Rows of trees grow in an apple orchard.

Growing and Picking Apples

Apple trees grow best in cooler places. In the United States, most apples grow in the north. Washington, Michigan, and New York are big apple growers. Apple trees are grown in large plantings called orchards. Most applesauce is made from fruit grown in orchards.

Caring for an apple orchard is a year-round job. Before the trees blossom in spring, apple farmers are at work. In spring, apple farmers plant new trees. A tree starts to produce apples when it is four or five years old.

A farmer plants a tree in an apple orchard.

Apple blossoms turn into apples.

A large orchard may grow many kinds of apples. Some apples are tart. Some apples are sweet. Some can be cooked into applesauce quickly. Others keep their shape better when they are cooked. Those apples are good for pies. Every apple starts with an apple blossom.

An apple begins to grow when the petals fall off the blossoms. In the United States, that usually happens in late spring. Apple farmers hope for the right mix of rain, warmth, and sunshine. Good weather makes apples grow bigger.

Many apples grow on a healthy apple tree.

Apple trees need water to grow.

During the summer, the apples ripen. Apple farmers are busy. They may have to water the trees. They check the trees for insects and diseases. Near harvest time, orchard owners hire people to pick the apples.

More than seven thousand kinds of apples grow around the world. When it is winter in North America, apples grow in the southern half of the world. People pick apples somewhere in the world all through the year.

Grocery stores carry apples all year.

Picking apples can be fun.

Most apples grown in the United States are picked in fall. August, September, and October are busy harvest times. Apples are usually picked by hand. They are placed in large bins. One good picker can pick up to 5,000 pounds (2,268 kilograms) of apples a day!

A forklift truck carries away the bins full of apples. Workers sort out the damaged apples. Good apples are sent to grocery stores.

A worker takes out damaged apples.

Can you find the apples that will become juice or applesauce?

Some good apples have marks on their skins. Others have odd shapes. These apples would not sell well in a store. Trucks take them to a factory. They make good juice or applesauce.

Inside a Food Factory

Some farmers use chemicals to get rid of insects.
At the factory, machines clean the apples.
Workers test to make sure no chemicals remain.

A machine washes the apples.

A machine peels the apples.

Machines peel, core, and slice the apples.
Another machine shreds and grinds the slices.
Do you like chunky or smooth applesauce?
Do you like it plain or flavored? Machines make
sure you get what you want.

The sauce is steam cooked so it will not spoil. Some of the applesauce may be mixed with strawberries, peaches, or other fruits. Then machines fill glass jars with applesauce. More applesauce is poured into little plastic cups. Each cup makes one healthy snack.

Each cup holds one serving of applesauce.

Applesauce snacks taste good.

The glass jars are placed in cardboard cartons.
The cartons protect the jars while they are
shipped. Trucks carry the cartons to grocery
stores. Customers can buy applesauce snacks
in many places.

Grocery workers stock the shelves. Stores have
many applesauce choices. Do you have a favorite?
It is fun to try out new kinds, too.

Applesauce is lined up on the grocery store shelf.

These cooks are about to make applesauce.

Making Applesauce at Home

Making applesauce is easy. Be sure to ask an adult for help. All you need are sliced apples and a little water. Most cooks cut out the seeds first. If the apples are tart, a little sugar can sweeten them. Cook the apples gently until they are soft.

Try making your own applesauce. Look for other special flavors, too. Any way you try it, applesauce tastes like a treat!

Homemade applesauce is a yummy treat!

Glossary

bins — storage containers

cartons — containers that are used to store or ship goods

chemicals — substances used to cause an effect, such as protecting fruit from disease or insects or making trees produce better fruit

core — the center part of a fruit

forklift truck — a machine that can pick up and carry a load

orchards — areas of land where fruit trees are grown

shreds — cuts into small strips

stock — to place a supply of something

tart — having a sharp or sour taste

For More Information

Books

Flanagan, Alice K. *The Zieglers and Their Apple Orchard*. NY: Children's Press, 1999.

Gibbons, Gail. *Apples*. NY: Holiday House, 2001.

Klingel, Cynthia Fitterer and Noyed, Robert B. *Apples. The Wonder of Reading* Series. Chanhassen, MN: Child's World, 2001.

Purmell, Ann. *Apple Cider Making Days*. Brookfield, CT: Millbrook Press, 2002.

Robbins, Ken. *Apples*. NY: Atheneum Books for Young Readers, 2002.

Web Sites

Apple Facts
applesonline.com/applefacts.cfm?first_time=1&id=3
Amazing facts unknown to most people

Apple Juice on the Internet
www.applejuice.org/
Activities and information about apple juice and apples

Le Crunch — French Apples
www.lecrunch.ie/pick.html
Facts, fun, and activities relating to apples

Index

About the Author

Gretchen Will Mayo likes to be creative with her favorite foods. In her kitchen, broccoli and corn are mixed with oranges to make a salad. She sprinkles granola on applesauce. She blends yogurt with orange juice and bananas. She experiments with different pasta sauces. When she isn't eating, Ms. Mayo writes stories and books for young people like you. She is also a teacher and illustrator. She lives in Wisconsin with her husband, Tom, who makes delicious soups. They have three adult daughters.